Praise for *A Day and Its Night*

"A genuine weightless joy." "George is one of my favorite thinkers of all time. This book is a remarkable invitation to listen—to both him and myself."

—Rachel Chavkin, Tony Award-Winning Director of *Hadestown*

"Beautiful, surprising, elegant, and funny truths... of which to be reminded. Or to learn."

—Katrina Lenk, Tony Award-Winning Actress

"A quiet plunge into the shimmering depth of George Abud's aphorisms and poems. Spacious, reflective, and quietly luminous. Each page offers a pocket of stillness, gently reminding us of what truly matters."

—Anne Bogart, Legendary Theatre Director & Author of *A Director Prepares*

"George Abud is a Renaissance man, a multi-disciplinary artist, and an uncommonly discerning human being. His peculiar brilliance permeates every page of *A Day and Its Night*—a delicate, comforting, and transformative piece of work."

—Joe Iconis, Tony Award-Nominated Composer of *Be More Chill*

"George takes the reader on a delicate ride with a sensibility squarely—and pleasurably—at odds with our era of 24-hour consumption. *Slow down*, the book seems to ask. Readers who do will be glad they did."

—Mona Mansour, Steinberg Award-Winning Playwright

A Day and Its Night
© 2025 George Abud

Published by Cogrounded, Inc.
325 E. Grand River Avenue
Suite 300
East Lansing, MI 48823
cogrounded.org

ISBN: 979-8-9919316-3-2 (paperback)
ISBN: 979-8-9919316-4-9 (hardcover)

Produced in the United States of America

Cover Design and Book Layout by Simone Meadows

Illustrations by Cecília Carollo
Typeset in Cormorant Garamond Regular, 12/14 pt

For more information from the author, please visit: georgeabud.com

For information about special discounts for bulk purchases, please contact: grow@cogrounded.org

Library of Congress Cataloging-in-Publication Data
Abud, George
A Day and Its Night / George Abud
5.5" x 8.5"
Poetry
Library of Congress Control Number: 2025946159

First Edition
2025

A DAY AND ITS NIGHT

aphorism advice and prose

BY GEORGE ABUD

"It is related of Chuang Tzu, the Chinese sage of the 4th century B.C., that when he was on his deathbed his disciples expressed the intention of giving him a burial worthy of his exalted station. His reply was: 'With Heaven and Earth for my coffin and shell; with the sun, moon, and stars as my burial regalia; and with all creation to escort me to the grave—are not my funeral paraphernalia ready to hand?'"

Mikhail Naimy

The Biography of Khalil Gibran

With deep gratitude to Paula Gaudier for her invaluable guidance in editing and clarifying these poems.

For Sebastian

.

Can a poem be just this?

It isn't that you do not know, it is that you are forgetful
And I have come to remind you.

There is no landing point just moments of beautiful exhalation

Never stop flooding your mind with that which inspires you

The driving force of life is not ambition but movement
We don't need to dominate but we must go

I find a boundless hopefulness
in the knowledge of how happy I can be
with so little

Is there no more beautiful color than the color of the sky right now?

Do trees have pure thoughts or are all things blemished?

Nothing will be better than right now

Good art doesn't capture a moment,
it frees it

You all know how the story ends
                         so how the hell are we going to get there?

Do nothing thinking it will impress someone,
because no one truly cares about what you're doing,
nor remembers it very long,
nor appreciates the complete meaning of it.

You must do and pursue only things that you love,
that you want,
that you think are worth doing.

And you must care deeply and alone.

Most seek their use to determine their self,
I seek myself to know my use.

The Purpose of Art

To Introduce
To Awaken
To Remind

To Unfold
To Reveal

To Release
To Slow Down

You get nervous
that
if you don't use enough words
and
don't hand it out on golden paper

you won't move people
they won't get your point

but when you
ever
get the point
yourself

it's usually a few words or so
covered in dust

sleeping on a skipped page

The Girl with the Flaxen Hair

There was a gentle man
standing next to a bench
on a particularly
beautiful
and simple day
and as easy as the breeze came
without looking my way
he told me a small story
about a girl with yellow hair
just for a few minutes
he told it in small pieces
as he seemed to need to collect himself
between bits
of breath and remembrance
she came into view
across a clear way
she walked shyly
and she held onto a small book
with her eyes cast down
and a smile upon her lips
and his too
and as she met his eyes
his breath ceased
and within him he reached to God in wonder
a small gust of wind
with a prayer of gratitude
how beautiful she was
a beauty
that made even him more beautiful
her smile grew
and his did too
and they began to walk
together
in opposite directions

passing
with some bright imprint on the others heart
of a bit of the sun's kiss

as he dropped his bow to his side
he smiled at me
and as he walked away
I looked up to God
and the yellow in the sun
leaned into me

and within me I repeated the story to my heart
she turned yellow
and offered herself
to God

Sighs are little bits of grace

Let learning often be unplanned

That you are here at all
is proof enough
that you are absolutely
necessary

Open your hands and make something of that which you hold

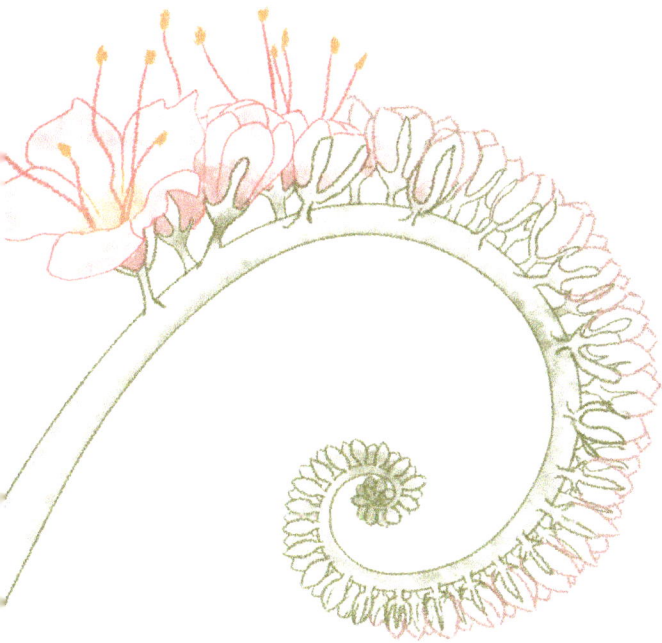

Tell me a story with no end
and please my darling,
speak slow

There is a beautiful unity
in hearing the same thing
in a new way

perhaps there is only one thing

Please.
Put this book down and come hold me
Hold me and read in my eyes all those wordless poems
I say to you in prayer each night

It is my fervent wish
That when I reach my end
I do not know all
That there is
To know

You do not need to have joy to express it

We are all indeed middle children between our past selves and our future selves.

Like plants we are,
needing to be repotted
in larger space or
new space,
with renewed soil,
sun,
air,
fragrance,
water,
and time.

Like plants,
we need nourishment beyond the walls
of our comprehension.

Is not all I see and all I wish to see the world?

How can your strings ever sound pleasing against a world that is out of tune?

Perhaps you wrote all of this for yourself at the very moment
you needed it

Why shall I continue to believe a sad day is without end and a happy one cannot last?

Emptiness stems not from a lack but from too much

I am always with myself.

The fingers and the instrument are lovers and the mind is very jealous.

I listen to Heifetz and Oistrakh play
La Fille Aux Cheveux De Lin
and they are both correct
but they have both seen a different girl
and she is both beautiful and distant

Art is a way for you to be there with people you don't know and for them to be with you

Theatre is the complete language of humanity

Be the greatest on a list of one.

I first began to read the poems of Mahmoud Darwish
in a new
old book I bought

On first skim,
I found it
impenetrable.

My thought was,
he doesn't translate well to English.
Or this translator is poor.
Or he is just unreachable.
or many things.

Until today.

I read the same words again,
this time slowly,
and seeking to understand.
I took my time and looked deep into the words and the spaces
It was revelatory

At first I demanded he be understandable to me

It was not until I came to him,
seeking to understand
to listen
to the way
he wished to communicate
with me

That I dove into the ocean of his pages
and have not come up for air

It will take you three hours to explain to your lover why you haven't had ten minutes to talk.

Each day
I become aware of
yet another
piece
of my life
for which
I
have been
ungrateful

How I admire the one who is tough
and pity the one who is hard,
for the tough fights for vulnerability
while the hard does everything possible to conceal theirs.

Look to what you provide your mind for its breakfast and supper
a poor diet is a poor diet.

It is sadly too often that our action betrays our intention
or perhaps it is our intention that betrays us

To give is to alleviate
not another
but yourself

So said my mother:
"Isn't it something to have been born at all and get to see the world?"

47

All art is telling

تقاسيم (*taqsim*) the arabic improvised solo

the note
detaching
existing
pure simple and alone
then beginning
to slowly gather
movement and shape around itself
then beginning
to branch out
in all directions
within a single mode
until
it finds elements and essences of
other modes
and begins entwining with those
it soars
yet seems always to be rooted
within the idea
of its original
note.

sometimes it goes very far away
from what it actually is
other times
it yearns to find its way back to its root
it lands
there
some times
and takes pause
and then it begins
again
with a new confidence
in itself
and plays with greater awareness
of its center

it more freely explores
new directions
the space and nuance
freedom
beauty
revelation
and
playfulness
within new modes
it marries with another
yet finds its way back
always
to its original

gracefully it lands
back
where it began
completing its journey
and releasing itself
the note
back into atmosphere
to be embraced within the great
sound
again
this time
with new

silence

The only one who is happy is he who believes he has enough

Are we not the passion of God?

A sense of wonder is the root of wisdom.

I saw an old woman walking up the long steps out of the
subway
and she was not struggling
she took one step
at a time
very slowly
with every bend of the leg.

I saw her
she bent down to grab something deliberately
even more slowly
it was an empty paper bag
she had a couple grocery bags
with not much in them

I rushed
up the other flight,
quietly
as I always do,
this time
to see if I should help her.

and in my haste
realized

perhaps I am the one
who needs

help.

As soon as you own it you lose it

Why should I tell you the next line of your poem?
Stop a minute finally and realize it.

In art
it does not matter
whether what you intended is what I receive
the point is that through your labor I recognize something
of my own
humanity

He who can't learn from one half his age is a fool.

I should only want to hear a good listener speak.
What would anyone else have to say?

There is no beauty in a choiceless decision

Why should I wake each day unless it be to ask myself
the same question and offer myself
a clearer response?

The deepest pain needs no outside help

The day I finally stopped asking for more I was given
all I could ever need.

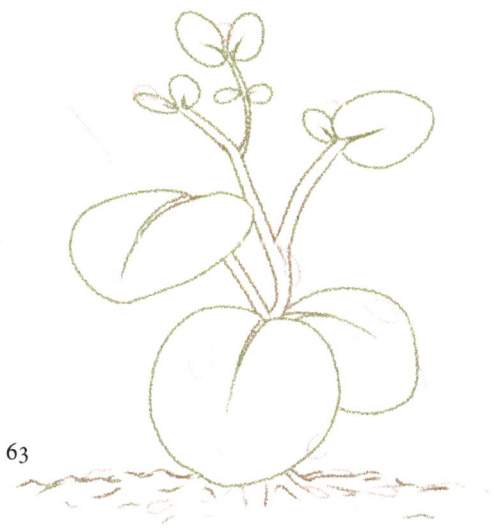

Teach me to speak and I shall teach you to sing

Every decision is born from feeling and in pursuit of feeling

a prayer of gratitude

to those
who
in their deepest pain
made of it
something
beautiful.

for if they
had not we
may forever have
succumbed to
ours.

a prayer of gratitude to those
who made
those smallest instruments of expression

words
notes
colors
limbs
sighs
silences

that we may fashion this image of ourselves and know we
are alive

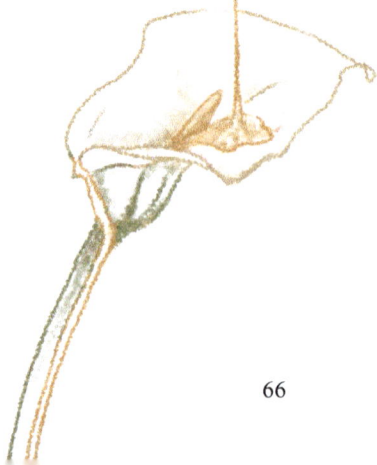

Art is something that needed to be said

.

Funny how falling in love
is far more painful
at times
than falling out

How is it from one instrument I hear two heartbeats?

There is only failure
There is no success.
For failure is an absence of trying not of success.
And success is but a myth wove to make you hate trying.

My cat
has not
checked his phone
once

Perhaps if I just explained to him how much it has to offer.

I do love nothing so much as consonants,
Save perhaps vowels.
The mountains and plains of a single word
And the word in search of its silence
And the silence in search of its word
Or perhaps it is your words
And your silences
Those mountains I gladly climb
and those plains
upon which I run to you
I do so love the geography
      of your speaking.

My fingers have only good memories
Would they would steer the ship

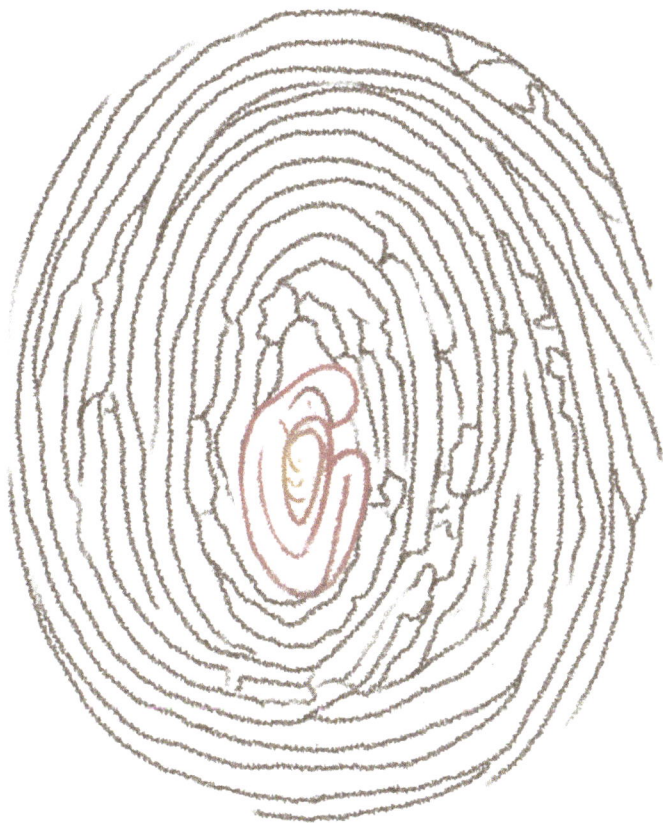

Art is the most accurate way of recording history

Life's parts do not add up to life
There is much more though you think it not so

Have respect for this day, it has fulfilled someone's life.
Have respect for this day, it has crumbled someone's heart.

Have respect for this day, you get to be in it and act
as the scales
between freedom

and ruin.

You have to take a full fucking breath.

The act of being human is reaching for something
with all your might, something that may never be there

But you must believe it to be.

Sit with me here and let us listen to the music that plays between our eyes

The theatre wonders at a thing a simple, pure, little thing.

A thing the world looks at and says, "oh that's a nothing."
The theatre says, "no that's a something."

The world stares at a person and says, "oh they're a no one,"
And the theatre says, "no they're a someone."

The world gawks at that which is unseen and unheard
and says, "that is nothing."

The theatre smiles, "my God, that is everything."

You own nothing
it is but your privilege to choose where next it is passed

Somehow God is more than what is, was, or shall be.

Those who rush are the slowest

Acting is like life in that you must have an understanding of the entire story from beginning to end, you must know all the characters and what they're going through, and you must know your purpose in the story, and then you must focus on the moment at hand and be unaware of the ending.

Telling is interesting
Trying to tell is more interesting

Is there much difference between those who refuse to take any blame and do nothing
and those who accept all blame and also
do nothing?

Only one who believes can convince.

I almost don't recognize a day without struggle
For when I play an oud with action too good
it never quite sounds like
an oud.

When I find
I do not
yet
understand something
uttered
by someone
wise

I know I have but
to wait
until I
am
there

perhaps
I don't even need to be
there

Words are the building blocks of image
And image is the foundation of words

Rolling the dice harder doesn't help the outcome
just guide their way and   boom

Who gives a fuck about the 27 year old?

Who stays up alone,
late hours,
and speaks words aloud
as if
he is having a conversation with his soul.
Who paces,
searching
searching for a reason not to go to bed
just wanting tomorrow to be now
not wanting to take the journey
who opens the fridge more than 5 times
who sits down
and perhaps looks at nothing
for long enough
until the urge
to reopen the fridge
this time to have pickles
to eat over the sink
and perhaps
for the first time
in the entire day
he breathes
cause he has finally stopped
staring at the wall past the sink
under the cupboards
chewing as loudly as he wishes
he eats the first one very fast
because he wants the second
and he devours the second one
because he has already decided
that he will have only three.
shaking them off a bit
so as not
to drop any brine on his bare toes

putting the jar away
it is the most important event
he has executed
in the five hours
between 10 pm and 3
he is still untired
and unsure
of tomorrow being worth the sleep
or today being finished

when do you know
that today
is

finished?

It's not why we're here it's what happens to us while we're here

I used to be scared of
escalators
but now

I'm not.

Ain't that some shit?

Those ruled by bitterness seek to invalidate the feelings of the joyous in order to satisfy their unquenchable emptiness.

I have no enemy save that which is common

How can you say we're talking when someone else is answering all your questions?

You must endeavor to love yourself
that is the main thing
you must love yourself.

If you're a shithead you'll need to correct that first.

He who would speak of a trophy before a flower has wasted much of his life

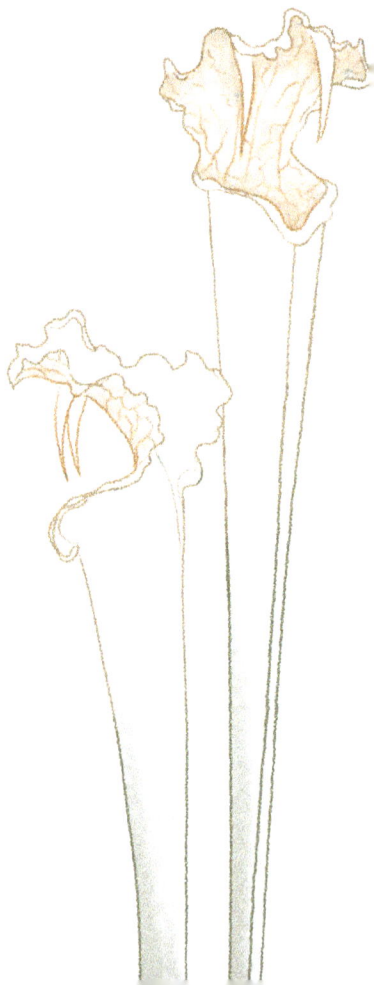

Would they could bomb a song,
raze a poem,
render a memory obsolete, they would.
How little they know of the earth, the winds,
and the roots of the trees.

A great artist does not bid me worship at their altar but rather at the altar of clarity.

I will believe you hear me when I see that you do

One who blames lives in a house with no mirrors.

In dreams one kiss on your lover's cheek is enough
In reality a thousand leave you wanting.

I think it would be nice not to care what my face looks
like when I look at you
that you would recognize in my look
how much I dream of you
and that would make me wholly un-selfconscious.

I don't know what you'll want of me
I have such a picture of you
And it's not of any face or body
but this ache in my chest my arms my chin
of being almost paralyzed in wanting
to receive you.

I want you
to banish my thoughts
of anything
but
you when we're near.
And when we're far.
I want each time you kiss me to be
a surprise.
And I want to die
from too much surprising.

And I want you
when you look at me
to not think about what
your face looks like.

Because our souls
are not concerned
with silly expressions
laugh lines or veins
or teeth or...

I miss you
without even knowing you.

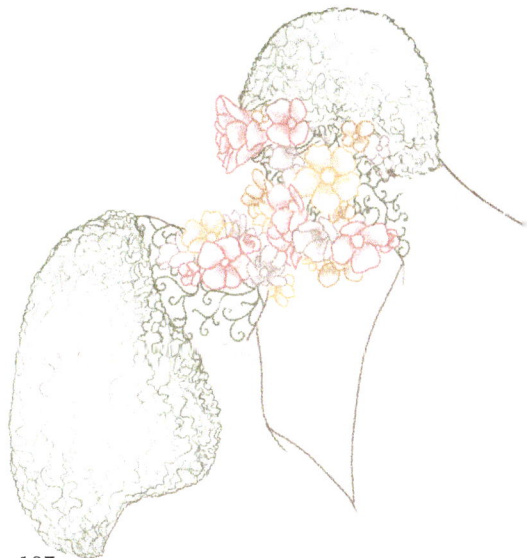

I have yet to find a correlation between age and wisdom.

Maybe if we all shut the fuck up long enough
we'd finally hear the answer

To find clarity in yourself is to find clarity for the world

Love others more than your self
And love yourself the most

They not only want you to tolerate this prison, they want you to love it.

It is considered a mismanagement of funds to give to those in need without requiring something in return

Life is not like the movies or a story in your book there is no one watching you no one investing in your aloneness and all your little feelings those momentous times in your life love and death and all that are not accompanied by a swelling orchestra or an omniscient voiceover or followed by a lens for all to see nor even afforded the proper space or time or circumstance you may be quite alone quite alone somewhere unseen and unheard you may be constantly interrupted you may have to fight to even allow the thing to happen and the thing could be so small it may fit in the palm of your hand and if you wait for the music to play or for the close-up or for the audience to hold their breath you may miss the greatest event that ever played out in front of you or within you the most wondrous times be they beautiful or tragic or otherwise could be occuring right now open your heart and look and you will hear that silent music

A point of blame is not a point of completion
but a dead end

Art is the opposite of a gun as a gun can only take away and art replenishes

Only the fulfilled have ceased seeking to be satisfied,
While the satisfied still seek fulfillment
but on the wrong path.

I had never been so bored till I went looking into other peoples' lives.

Always be weary of the interrupter
They have nothing to say who need say it before the
other is finished.

No one will ever have my thinking

Intelligence is a collection of facts, wisdom is a collection of silences
Intelligence bids you listen to it, wisdom begs you listen with it

the women at the vineyard

How I pity them
for you see
they think they have it all
How I pity myself
for I have everything
and I know it not

Happiness and satisfaction are not destinations

Believe in yourself as God did when He trusted that small piece of His own spirit to make alive this body of yours.

Would that we'd fight as hard to live as not to die

Seek always to understand
but not immediately

Have not all lovers uttered the same words throughout
time without knowing
they discovered those words?

I aspire to nothing

Those who worry about me
and forsake themselves
do me little good

The opportunity you're most scared of is usually something quite meaningful to you. Instead of worrying about it and trying to get it over with, try enjoying the damn thing. And know that even though you're nervous you'll get through it somehow. Most likely it will go wonderfully and you'll be back at home in your bed before you know it, safe. And you'll think, can we go again?

The worst thing that can happen is you die, and if you die then you don't have to worry about anything.

They want my name and the way I look but they don't want my voice

Never break up the set.

You will have lived when you look
out the window of a car
on a sun-drenched day and see
a man hosing down the few feet of sidewalk outside his store

and a woman walking past
then sharply turning around,
then looking up at the corner realizing she has gone
the wrong way

and a small child singing
in such a way that no one would call
music

You will have lived when you see these things
and it excites you
for these are the building blocks of living

The fragments of a day in which one is too consumed
with participating to consider as something regal and
consequential and fulfilling and real

These are the moments the actor wishes to represent
the meaningless
the unimportant
the less than great
the in-between
the usual
the mundane
the small

The actor sees these things and says,
ah that is life and that is living
and how I will portray them in such a way
that one who is not an actor shall see them and say,
that is me and ah
I have lived.

To measure the man, look to his end and the quality of those
who show up with nothing to gain but the privilege of being there

Perhaps...
music is a woman
who speaks in a way
that men can only
long
to comprehend

It is not morning til the pink that sleeps on her lips
rises in her cheek.

What should your days be like if the clouds were your earth and the infinite your view?

Is not that shattering silence but an answer from God?

I work very hard to protect this being that tortures me most

The worst are the hypocrites and we are all hypocrites.

I have known an ecstasy so vivid that I would spend each moment here forward helping you seek it

Keep me talking baby
Keep me in my lips and in my breath
And out of my mind

It is interesting the term fall in love seems to have need of two people but I fell in love last night. not with anyone. not with myself. not with any thing. but my heart fell in love. an ocean of it. and it swelled and made me breathe bigger and with more sensations. and I just laid there eyes wide as I seemed to let my heart have this moment this beautiful moment. and I felt such joy for my heart that it fell in love. and my eyes had tears. and it took me a while to come down from it and finally sleep. it was that same rush. it's still singing in there
a little. the same song. the same song.

Truly it is never the word, it is the utterer
The word is the meeting point.

How many days shall I renew this heartbreak?

Perhaps there is envy for the needy by the needless.

Only a great artist leads me to the understanding that greater art is still to come.

To those 6 birds on the telephone line in Salt Lake City
Do you know that you're in Utah?
Do you even think about New York?
Is a good sit plenty for you?
And a good view?
Cause you've certainly got it
and your pals with you

Do you ever get tired of your pals?

You never remember how long a day is

until the day

you do

He who would deny my faith has no faith

I sat inside the church today and God stood outside

Music lets me ride upon time rather than be crushed by it

I know how hard it is
I know
but please
try to sing
the entire
song

The later verses, I promise you, are the most beautiful.

Near impossible is not impossible and impossible
has only been so til now

I don't know what I wish but I do wish it

It's painful to admit
to myself
that there is only one
of you
that there is no one else like you

As I scour the streets
the skies
the windows
and the tree tops
for that hair
and volcano cheek
those legs
and that soul

Why would God be so cruel
out of all people
to make you
a limited edition

I don't want the duplicate
I don't want the richer
or
the freer you
I just want
the peace
knowing
that
it wasn't you
all
along

But I fear
my darling
I am
wrong

155

The kindness of man can be observed in how he listens to he whom no one else cares to listen.

If you don't tell me of where you are
it could be lost forever

Funny you should think it an unnecessary part of the story

The pain you feel is not
the whole
but rather
a small part
of the world's greater pain

you carry it in union with all creatures

consider it a day's work
rather than
a night's burden

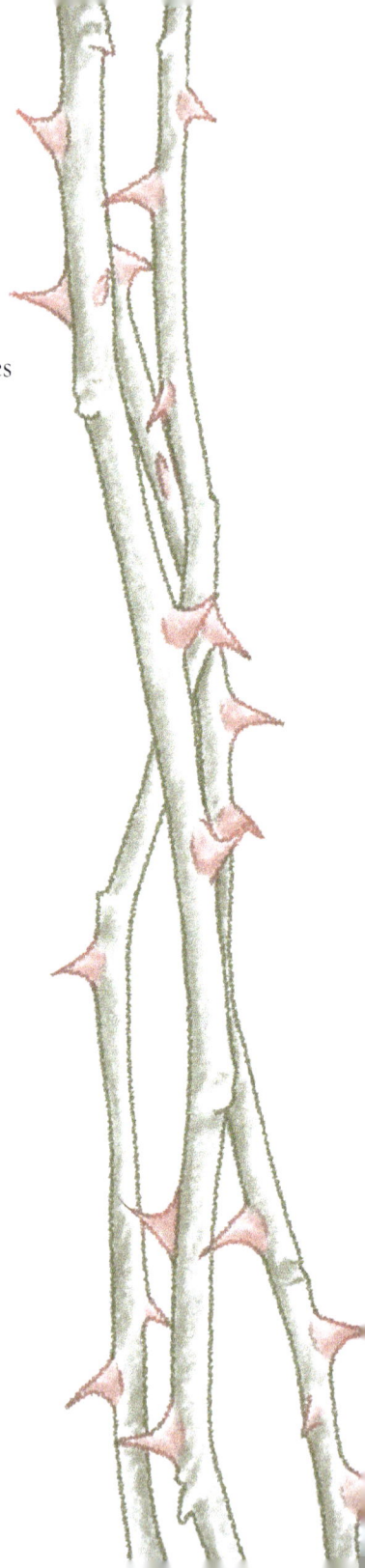

Perhaps the only justice is the strength not to require justice.

You may spend your whole life to give another but one moment of lasting joy, and would not that be a life well lived?

How you are going is where you are going

Reach till your fingers touch the thing you seek

If this isn't it, what is?

How could I love God and be out of love with myself
when all I am is of God?

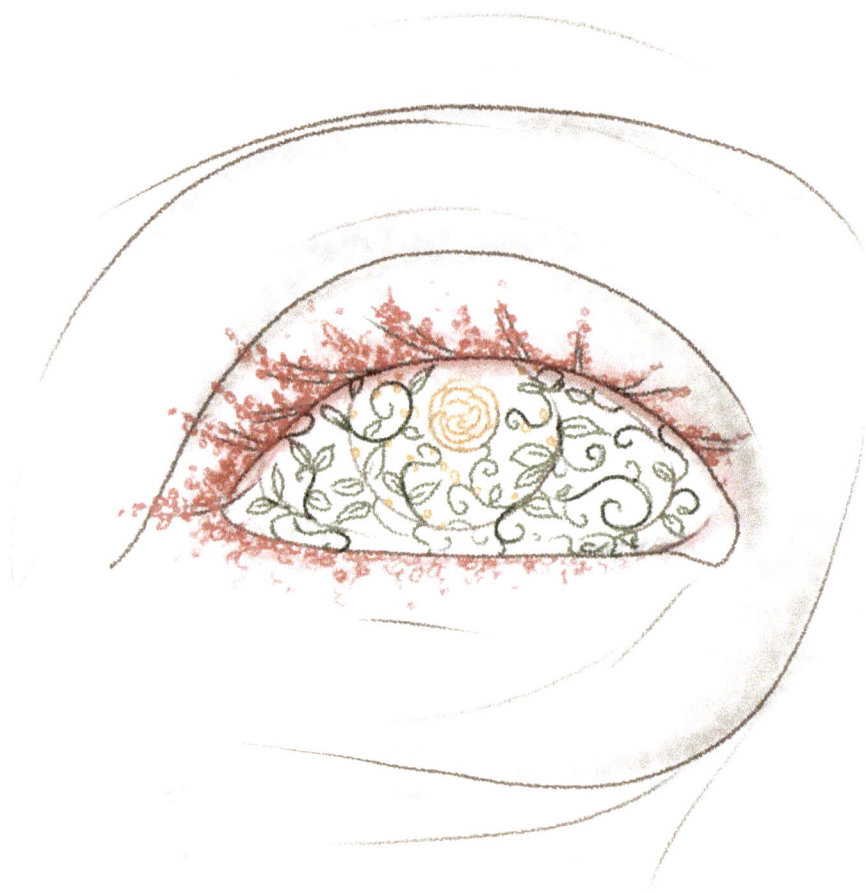

If you could but see the tears that stained the paper you might better know the cost of the words.

There's something unbelievably brave about choosing to sleep at night and choosing to wake in the morning.

You would clothe in words a feeling unashamed of its own nakedness.

If only you could see yourself from without yourself
you wouldn't envy or wage war

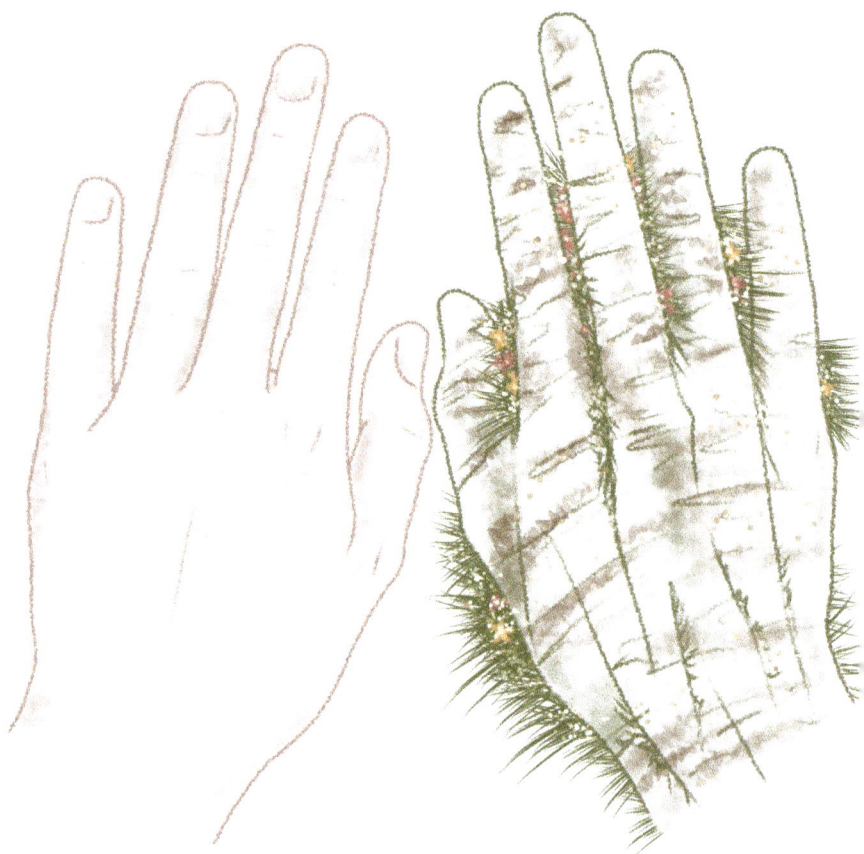

It began to rain outside my window
there are two of them
that look out onto some other buildings
and sky and moon
very serene in the late night
and I played the Oud
and God said, take it easy
it's okay
it's okay
Everyone slept
and I played
a common occurence
I like it
I feel they can feel safe
cause I'm awake
and I played
and Sebastian slept in his little house
right across from me
and it made me happy
that he felt safe
so many unsafe out there
outside that window

nice
that there are a few
at least right now
that do not feel that
as I play

the newborn bears the answer   the aged seeks the question

What an accomplishment to have attained a loving disposition

What an unconsidered accomplishment.

Go and find it
and say it back
in a way that
is absolutely clear
to you.

If you could feel as I do when I play but one note with
utter clarity you would let go
your ambitions,
your comforts,
your philosophies
and place your hand on mine.

Don't rush

The sky is always there, but it is not always pink, and it is not always this pink, and it is not always ravishingly beautiful. In truth, it is perhaps only for a moment now and then, and it stops you. And you feel something about it. And something else in the sky grabs you again another day but it is not that same pink, but it is a yellow. And it is ravishingly beautiful. But yellow feels different than pink. And pink different than yellow. Both were there. And you were there. And now they're both gone. And perhaps you are gone too. But the important thing is you stopped. You must stop. And if you don't think that the color of that one sky is enough to stop, then when would you ever stop?

a poem at 3 a.m. in January

She wrote a poem upon my eyes with her sleeping face
And with each short breath
she extended the world one more day one more day

She brought me to bed through my sleepless hours and there
Wrote a poem upon my breath
And made me long to wake one more day one more day

Late that night I played the Oud alone
and all the alchemies that needed to visit my hands
and my voice came to me
and I played perhaps the best I had ever played
my whole life

and as the thought struck
that I should be disappointed that no one heard my
triumph

God quickly revealed His truth:

I heard it

and that was more than enough

perhaps that was all.

There is something unusually powerful about the empty space that falls beneath the final words on a final page

GEORGE ABUD

Abud's lifework as an artist spans the disciplines of acting, directing, music, and writing. As actor, he has appeared on the Broadway Stage in the landmark musicals, *Lempicka*, *The Band's Visit*, and *The Visit*; the recipient of a Daytime Emmy Award, as well as a nominee for the prestigious Drama Desk Award for Outstanding Actor in a Musical. As playwright, his premiere work *The Ruins* received its world premiere production at the legendary Guthrie Theater in Minneapolis, Minnesota. Descending from four generations of Lebanese Oud players, Abud has been a frequent soloist at the United Nations, as well as the first individual to play the Oud for the late legendary composer Stephen Sondheim. It was as director of the opera *Riders to the Sea* where he met his collaborator, Cecília Carollo, who has woven the exquisite visual poetry to embody his lines and verses.

A Day and Its Night, which comprises the aphorisms and poems of a young man in search of his soul, marks Abud's first volume of poetry.

CECÍLIA CAROLLO

Cecília Carollo, known artistically as Histerlia, is a Brazilian digital illustrator whose work is a reflection of self, fantasy, and poetry. With a deep love for artistic expression, her art evokes deep emotions; other times, it simply exists as a fleeting moment of beauty and magic.

With love, she feels honored to bring these poems to life, a tribute to the words of her dear friend, George Abud.

www.ingramcontent.com/pod-product-compliance
Lightning Source LLC
Chambersburg PA
CBHW051210090426
42740CB00022B/3455